DEATH OF AN ADULT CHILD

AND OTHER POEMS

MARYALICIA POST

Contents

Questions to which there can be no answer for the foreseeable future

When your road ran out
Did it end in dense fog or open
Out into bright sun on the shore
Of a blue-watered ocean? Were
Old friends waiting? Will you be waiting
For me? Or perhaps, as I sometimes feel,
Have you never left?

Conditional perfect..

Could have, would have
and should have
are sometimes called
"modals of lost opportunities"

Could have/
Would have/
Should have/
Three blows of an axe
The past cut adrift
Like a small boat
In fast-moving waters
First swept out of reach
Then lost to sight

The impossibility of writing a poem about the death of my daughter

I need words to glitter, to shine,
to carry my grief
like a richly encrusted chariot

To say she loved light,
green plants, wild birds
seashells

Hid her pills,
hid her pain,
sometimes

But her anger
her laugh or her love
never

And all I have to
contain this gift
is an undecorated box:

'I miss her'

Almost a Ghazal

Each morning I wait
Her chair stays empty

Are those her footsteps?
The hallway's empty

Grief rises like smoke
Fills my days, empty

It's not raining but still
There's a haze, empty

Moon lights her bed,
Though it lays empty

A pessimist looks at optimism

Optimism.. hope unlearned….
Believing
There's gold in the glint of paving stones
That toast will land butter side up
That my words will touch someone
That 'longing' is part of belonging
That pain will stop
This heart will heal

I am not here to make a scene but ....

I wish to register a death
I wish to make a complaint
I want to report a loss..
I want to poke a hole in
Heaven and scream a message through
To the other side
Yes register the loss.
The loss
To my world
A loss of beauty, laughter, love
I wish to complain about this
And have her restored
To me. At once.
My daughter. Who must I see?
What forms
Must I fill out? How do I register
This death? There must
Be something there is always
Something. Tell me.

Please

Tanka: absence

vacant rooms
her remembered shape
filling space
but what shall I do
about the silence

Death of an Adult Child

I wish she had died in her bed with
Her head on the pillowcase I bought her
When I could think of nothing else to ease
Her pain..
Blissy it was called

I wish she had died in my arms
The day she wept because time
Was passing and it was already afternoon
And she could neither stand up nor lie down
Then the ambulance came

I wish I had held her longer
The night she returned and I said
I am so glad you're home again
Not knowing
How soon she'd be leaving

I wish she hadn't
Lain on a cold tile floor
Comfortless til I found her
I wish she had died in her bed
With her head on the silk pillowcase.

Wishing you safe

So many years I've wished you safe
An infant swaddled in pink
A child reaching for my hand
A young woman hugging me fast
Her life waiting
And now
Your journey beginning
before mine
I wish you safe
As I always have, as I always will
Safe home

FINIS

Other books by this author

After You

Arc

This Life: a love story

Sky Full of Clouds

Website: maryaliciapost.com